CONTENTS

WHO'S GOING TO THE MUSEUM?

At last the exhibition is ready. Important people are here for the opening ceremony. The fabulous golden Mask of the Toltecs has been brought from Central America. Everyone is talking about it on the radio and TV. Thirty years ago, archaeologists found the mask hidden deep inside a pyramid. Now it is on display in the museum in the city where you live. Many people are working hard behind the scenes, both to allow visitors to enjoy the exhibition but also to keep the mask safe.

The story starts on Monday May 4th

FABULOUS TREASURE

Here is the Mask of the Toltecs. A thousand years ago, the Toltecs inhabited the Yucatan Peninsula, the thin strip of land which lies between North and South America. The Toltecs were a warlike people. They built huge pyramids, to honour their gods, with steps up the sides and temples at the top. Nobody today knows who made the Mask of the Toltecs or what it was originally used for.

PREPARED FOR TROUBLE

The **curator** is the person in charge of the museum. He has worked hard to make the exhibition exciting so that everyone will want to come to see the mask. The curator has also spent much time with the local police chief. He and the chief have agreed together how to keep the mask safe during its stay at the museum. If anything goes wrong with security, they have special plans to set into action.

Chief of Police

Curator

Mask

The curator and the daytime securit staff meet in the museum at 8.30am

BEHIND THE SCENES

SOLVING A CRIME

Written by Peter Mellett

Illustrated by Terry Riley

Heinemann
LIBRARY

First published in Great Britain by Heinemann Library, Halley Court,
Jordan Hill, Oxford OX2 8EJ, a division of Reed Educational and
Professional Publishing Ltd.
Heinemann is a registered trademark of Reed Educational & Professional
Publishing Limited.

OXFORD MELBOURNE AUCKLAND
IBADAN JOHANNESBURG BLANTYRE
GABORONE PORTSMOUTH NH (USA) CHICAGO

Produced for Heinemann Library by Lionheart Books, London.
Editor: Lionel Bender
Art Director: Ben White
Illustrated by: Terry Riley
Cover artwork: Roger Stewart
Page make-up: MW Graphics

Printed in Hong Kong by Wing King Tong

03 02 01 00 99
10 9 8 7 6 5 4 3 2 1

British Library Cataloguing in Publication Data
Mellett, Peter
Solving a Crime. - (Behind the scenes)
1.Forensic Science - Production and direction - Juvenile literature
I.Title
791.4'3'0232

ISBN 0 431 02166 X

Acknowledgements
Every effort has been made to contact copyright holders of any
material reproduced in this book. Any omissions will be rectified in
subsequent printings if notice is given to the Publisher.

Any words appearing in the text in bold, **like this**, are explained in
the Glossary.

OUTSIDE ACTIVITY

Builders are repairing part of the roof of the museum. They are also adding an extension at one end. Powerful earth-moving machines dig trenches in the ground. The machines are fitted with simple ignition keys so that any workmen can use them.

SECURITY

The chief **security officer** is in charge of the guards who make sure everything in the museum is kept safe. The guards patrol through the museum day and night and have electronic alarms and TV cameras to help their work.

Chief of Security

The TV team arrive at 12.30 to set up their equipment.
The building site is closed down so that sounds do not disturb the ceremony

ON DISPLAY

The mask is enclosed in a glass display cabinet. Within the base of the cabinet is an electronic alarm unit that is wired up to a security **control room** in the museum.

MYSTERY AND THE MASK

Radio, TV and newspapers have all been telling the famous story of the Mask of the Toltecs. The archaeologists who took it from the pyramid all suffered mysterious deaths. Some people say that wearing the mask brings misfortune.

KEEPING THINGS SAFE

Every part of the museum is carefully monitored for 24 hours each day. Security staff regularly patrol inside the building. They use walkie-talkie radios to keep in contact with the control room. A guard sits in the control room watching TV screens connected to cameras in every room. Burglar alarms are fitted to doors and windows. At night, alarms ring if an intruder just walks across a room. Smoke alarms are fitted in rooms and in corridors.

Alarm switch on door

Beam of infra-red light

At night, just two security staff guard the whole building

SECURITY DEVICES

The exhibition room is fitted with extra **surveillance equipment**. Open the door and a hidden switch closes, setting off warning lights in the control room. There are also invisible beams of infra-red light which guard the exhibits. Walk through a beam or try to open the display cabinet containing the mask and the alarm will ring.

DOOR SWITCHES

Each door switch relies on magnetism to work. There is a magnet inside the door and a special '**reed switch**' hidden in the door frame. When the door is closed, the magnet attracts a steel strip inside the switch. Opening the door moves the magnet. The strip springs back, touching an electrical contact that switches on the warning light in the control room.

Door closed

Door open – alarm goes off

Magnet

Steel strip

Reed switch

Each door has a reed switch linked back to the control room

SECURITY GUARDS

Each security guard carries a walkie-talkie radio. It contains a battery-powered receiver and a transmitter with a range of 500 metres. To talk, the guard presses the 'Send' button and speaks into the microphone at the front of the unit. A 'pip' tone sounds when there is an incoming message. The guard then presses the 'Receive' button and puts the front of the unit to one ear. A tiny loudspeaker converts the electric signals into sounds that can be heard.

Infra-red rays travel at 300,000 kilometres/second – about 1 million times faster than a rifle bullet

ALARM

In an emergency, a guard can press a special button on a walkie-talkie so that the unit sends out a signal that rings the alarm.

A LIGHT TRAP

The Toltec mask cabinet is guarded by invisible beams of light. Special lamps give off **infra-red rays**, which our eyes cannot see. The rays criss-cross the room like bars in a prison. Each ray shines into a **sensor** linked to the control room. Break any beam and the sensor rings the alarm.

INFRA-RED RAYS?

Infra-red rays are a type of energy made up from electric and magnetic vibrations travelling through space. This 'electromagnetic' energy includes radio waves, infra-red rays, visible light, and the X-rays doctors use to photograph inside your body. Infra-red rays are beamed from the handset you use to change the channel on your TV.

Walkie-talkie unit   *Panic button*   *Send button*   *Receive button*   *Aerial*

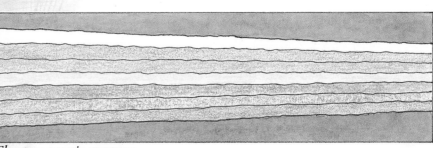

Electromagnetic spectrum

NIGHT-TIME RAID

It happened at 3:30 am. in the middle of the night. The first thing the guards heard was the roar of the digging machine's engine. Next, there was a crash as the digger's steel shovel smashed through the window of the exhibition room. Guards raced into the room but were beaten back by clouds of billowing smoke. Later, when the air had cleared, the guards discovered two burnt-out smoke grenades on the floor. The glass cabinet was open and the mask had disappeared. The guards at once called the curator and the chief of police.

The robbery happens at 3.30am. The guard in the control room sees the smashed window on the TV monitor

DON'T PANIC!

Immediately the mask is stolen, the museum responds to a pre-arranged plan. Each person knows exactly what to do. Together they must catch the thief and recover the mask. The plan swings into action.

Chief of Police

Museum curator

Chief of museum security

THREE PHONE CALLS

The chief of police is calling for teams of **detectives** to come quickly. One team will search for **clues** while another team will ask the museum staff questions. The curator is telephoning the insurance loss-adjuster. If the mask is not found, the insurance company must pay $10 million to the owners in South America. The chief of museum security calls for all the records from the control room. They will show when doors opened and closed and where the guards were patrolling. There may be important clues recorded from the surveillance cameras.

The insurance loss-adjuster is woken by the curator's call.

INSURANCE

The loss-adjuster will ensure that everything is done to recover the mask and that no **fraud** is involved. Each year, the owners of the mask pay an 'insurance premium' of $10,000 to the company.

He phones the police and then the curator at 3.34am

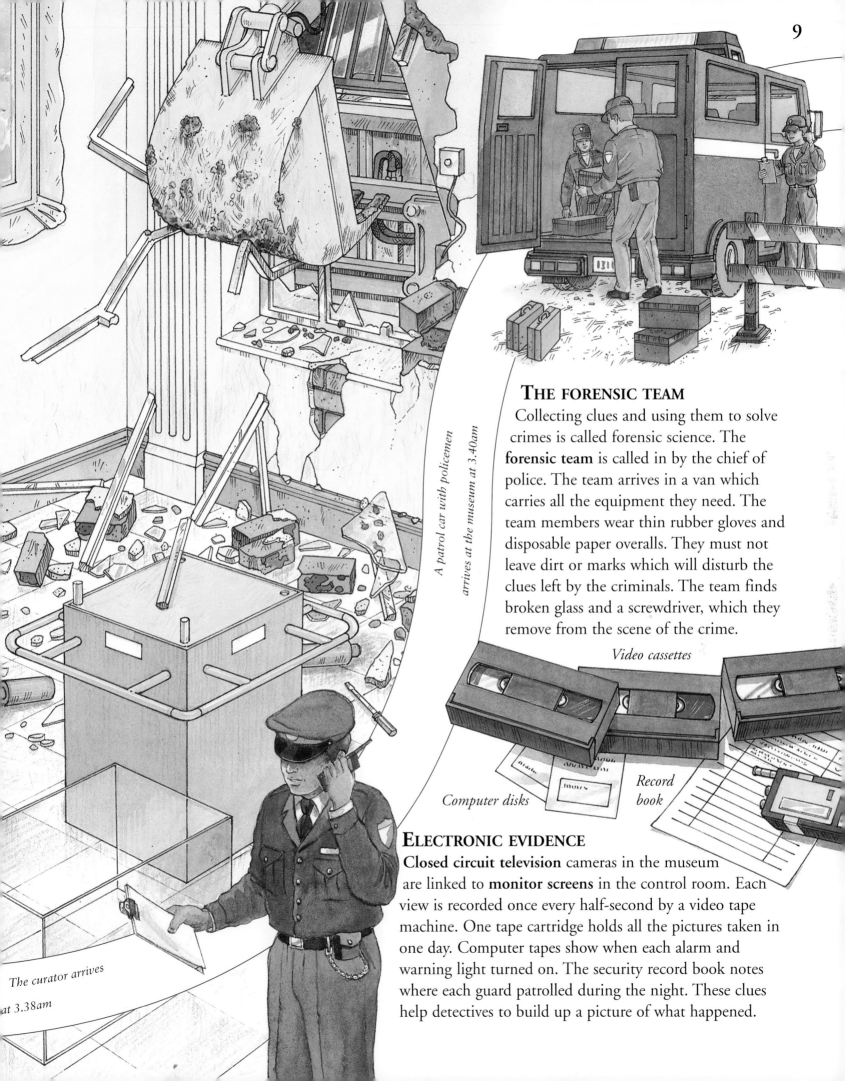

A patrol car with policemen arrives at the museum at 3.40am

The curator arrives at 3.38am

THE FORENSIC TEAM

Collecting clues and using them to solve crimes is called forensic science. The **forensic team** is called in by the chief of police. The team arrives in a van which carries all the equipment they need. The team members wear thin rubber gloves and disposable paper overalls. They must not leave dirt or marks which will disturb the clues left by the criminals. The team finds broken glass and a screwdriver, which they remove from the scene of the crime.

Video cassettes

Computer disks

Record book

ELECTRONIC EVIDENCE

Closed circuit television cameras in the museum are linked to **monitor screens** in the control room. Each view is recorded once every half-second by a video tape machine. One tape cartridge holds all the pictures taken in one day. Computer tapes show when each alarm and warning light turned on. The security record book notes where each guard patrolled during the night. These clues help detectives to build up a picture of what happened.

WHAT DID YOU HEAR OR SEE?

Detectives interview the curator and the other museum staff, asking them questions and carefully noting down all the answers. "Our aim, sir, is to put together a picture of the events leading up to and surrounding the crime." Nobody is allowed to leave the building until they have told their story. "When did you enter the museum? Where did you go? What did you see? What was the time then?" By comparing the different stories, detectives work out what probably happened during the robbery.

THE FIRST SECURITY GUARD'S STORY

"... I was patrolling the corridor outside the exhibition room. At 3:30 am. I heard the sound of the digger's engine. Twenty seconds later there was a great crash as it broke through the window and bars. I ran to the room and pushed the doors open. There was smoke everywhere. I couldn't see a thing. Alarms were ringing...."

3.30am. Guards hear the digger engine

The police detective interviews the curator and a security guard.

INITIAL INTERVIEWS

The mask was stolen less than two hours ago and now the museum is swarming with detectives. They must quickly interview all members of the museum staff while their memories are still fresh as to what they were doing at 3.30 am. and what, if anything, unusual did they notice at the time.

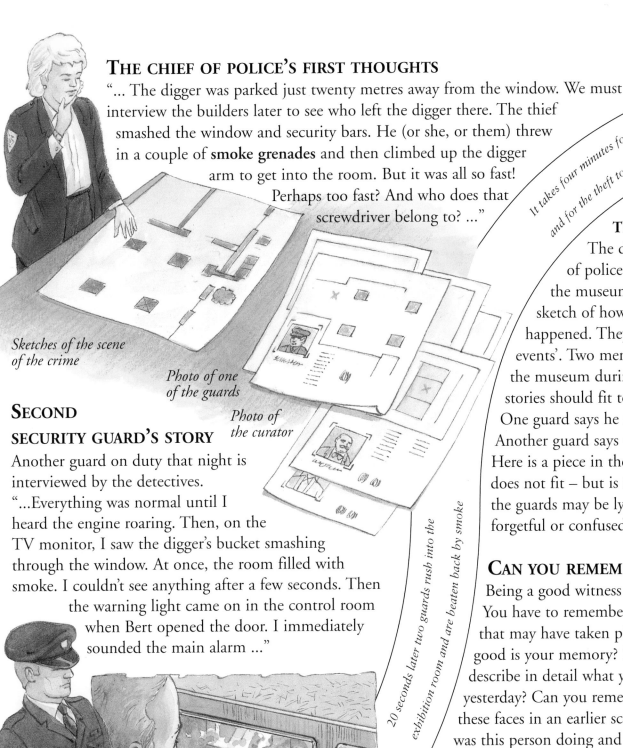

THE CHIEF OF POLICE'S FIRST THOUGHTS

"... The digger was parked just twenty metres away from the window. We must interview the builders later to see who left the digger there. The thief smashed the window and security bars. He (or she, or them) threw in a couple of **smoke grenades** and then climbed up the digger arm to get into the room. But it was all so fast! Perhaps too fast? And who does that screwdriver belong to? ..."

Sketches of the scene of the crime

Photo of one of the guards

Photo of the curator

SECOND SECURITY GUARD'S STORY

Another guard on duty that night is interviewed by the detectives.
"...Everything was normal until I heard the engine roaring. Then, on the TV monitor, I saw the digger's bucket smashing through the window. At once, the room filled with smoke. I couldn't see anything after a few seconds. Then the warning light came on in the control room when Bert opened the door. I immediately sounded the main alarm ..."

It takes four minutes for the smoke to clear and for the theft to be discovered

20 seconds later two guards rush into the exhibition room and are beaten back by smoke

20 seconds later the digger hits the building

FITTING THINGS TOGETHER

The detectives and the chief of police use the **statements** of the museum staff to make a quick sketch of how the robbery may have happened. They call it 'the sequence of events'. Two members of staff were in the museum during the robbery. Their stories should fit together and agree.
One guard says he made coffee at 03.20. Another guard says the time was 03.00. Here is a piece in the jigsaw puzzle that does not fit – but is it important? One of the guards may be lying, or he may just be forgetful or confused by the speed of events.

CAN YOU REMEMBER?

Being a good witness to a crime is not easy. You have to remember every detail of events that may have taken place in seconds. How good is your memory? For example, can you describe in detail what you were doing this time yesterday? Can you remember seeing one of these faces in an earlier scene in this book? What was this person doing and who was he or she standing next to? (Now check page 4 to see if you were correct.)

SEARCHING FOR CLUES

The forensic team painstakingly looks for clues that may have been left behind by the burglars. They photograph the scene from all angles and then carefully search the whole exhibition room. They collect fingerprints, hairs, dust and particles of soil. Detectives check the clues against the evidence they have, and try to fit them with the statements from the museum staff. Only some of the clues are useful and help to build up a full picture of what happened. If the criminals are finally caught, these clues can be used as evidence to prove that they are guilty.

Tuesday May 5th 8.30am. The forensic team have set up all their equipment and start work

8.30 – 9.00 am. Taking photographs

9.00 am – 6.30 pm. Searching for clues

COLLECTING FINGERPRINTS

One of the **forensic scientists** dusts fine powder on the glass case. The powder sticks to invisible **fingerprints** and makes them show up. The scientist uses clear sticky tape to 'lift' the fingerprints. The dusty pattern clings to the tape, which is then stuck onto a plastic sheet. All the collected fingerprints are taken back to the police station for examination.

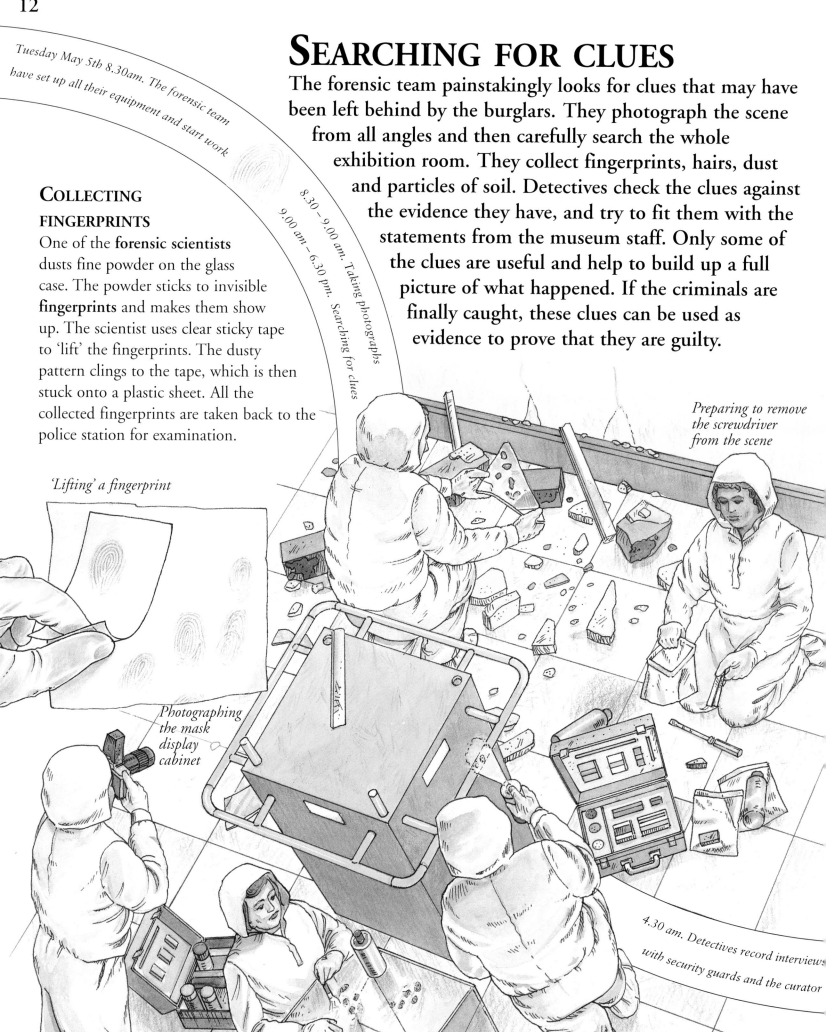

'Lifting' a fingerprint

Photographing the mask display cabinet

Preparing to remove the screwdriver from the scene

4.30 am. Detectives record interviews with security guards and the curator

FINGERPRINT PATTERNS

The skin on your hands is folded into tiny creases. Between the creases are sweat glands which make the skin slightly damp. Touching a smooth surface leaves behind a fingerprint – an invisible copy of the skin creases. Each person has their own distinctive set of fingerprints. There are three main patterns or types – loops, arches, and whorls.

Loop   *Arch*   *Whorl*

The three main types of fingerprint

... the written statements are read through with each person to make sure they are accurate

Making a plaster cast of the footprint

COLLECTING FOOTPRINTS

There are footprints in the soft earth around the digger. A forensic scientist puts a plastic trough around each footprint and pours in liquid plaster to completely cover the footprint. The plaster hardens to make a copy of the footprint called a **plaster cast**. It shows all the marks on the sole of the shoe and sometimes can reveal how the person walks. One cast is very strange and has a distinctive wavy pattern on the heel. The shoe was made in Central America by the El Castillo Boot Company. These shoes are not sold in this country.

The sole of the El Castillo boot

A MICROSCOPIC VIEW

Soil is made from a mixture of humus, clay, and sand. Humus is plant remains which have rotted into a sort of compost. Clay particles are extremely small; sand grains are larger. Soil mixtures vary from place to place.

SOIL SAMPLES

Tiny particles of soil will have stuck to the burglar when he or she climbed up the digger arm. This forensic scientist is collecting a soil sample. If a suspect is caught later, samples taken from their clothes, finger nails and shoes may match the soil from around the museum. A match is strong **evidence** that the person was at the museum.

Recorded interviews are typed out...

Sand grain

Humus

Clay particle

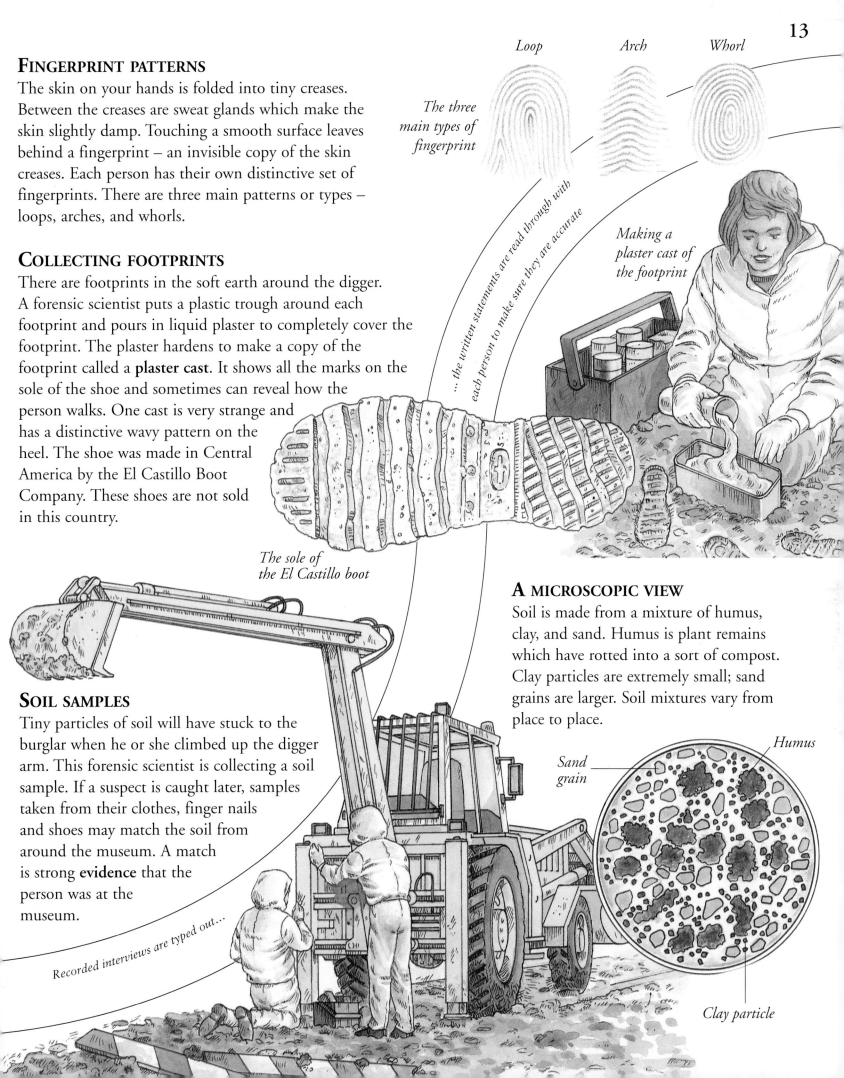

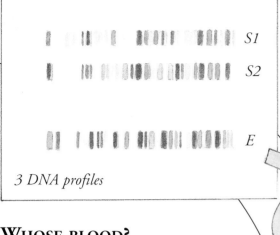

3 DNA profiles

ANALYZING THE CLUES

Without realizing it, criminals usually leave behind hairs, fragments of skin and even blood. Our bodies are made from billions of tiny units called cells. Inside every cell is a coiled-up chemical called DNA. This substance controls how our bodies work and what we look like. Except for identical twins, no two people have the same DNA. Scientists can use anything which comes from a human body to make a pattern called the DNA profile. Just a few cells are enough to make a DNA profile. Cells collected at the exhibition room incident will be examined in a science laboratory.

WHOSE BLOOD?

Here is the **DNA profile** made from the drops of blood. No matter what part of a person is used to make the profile, it will always contain the same pattern of lines. The profiles from different people have lines in different places. When the police catch a suspect, they will compare the DNA profile of that person with the profile of the blood from the glass fragment.

A laboratory technician separates the DNA from the rest of the blood.

DNA molecules look like twisted ladders.

A LUCKY FIND

Underneath the smashed window frame of the exhibition room was a pile of dusty broken glass. On one jagged fragment was a tiny red streak which looked like blood. The forensic detective put the glass into a plastic box, which she then carefully labelled. At the laboratory, scientists will remove the streak from the glass, analyze the blood sample and make a DNA profile.

Spots of blood on the glass

Wednesday May 6th. The blood sample found yesterday arrives at the forensic laboratory 40 kilometres away. The results will not be ready until late tomorrow

VIDEO-TAPED CLUES

One of the forensic scientists rewinds the exhibition room videotape than presses the 'fast forward' button on the video machine to view the tape quickly. He sees: 6.00 pm: the museum is closed. Then every 20 minutes the room door opens and a guard looks in. Nothing else happens for nine hours until –
3.01 am: the door is closed.

3.20 am: the door opens and a guard checks the room.
3.30 am plus 20 seconds: the digger crashes through the window.
3.30 plus 40 seconds: thick smoke fills the room.
3.34 plus 40 seconds: the smoke clears revealing the smashed and empty showcase and two coughing guards.

COMPARING PROFILES

Here are two sets of DNA profiles: one connected with the theft of the mask, the other with another robbery. The profile labelled E was made from the root of a hair found at the scene of the crime. The profiles S1 and S2 come from two suspects the police arrested. Can you see a match between two sets?

S1

S2

E

Forensic scientists hope soon to crack the code so they can tell what a suspect looks like from a sample of their DNA

The letters DNA stand for deoxyribose nucleic acid. We look like our parents because the DNA in our cells contains a code inherited from each of them

CHECKING THE ELECTRONICS

Electronics experts are called in to check TV cameras, door switches and **infra-red beams**. It is important to know that all the security equipment was working properly when the robbery happened. The experts make sure these sensors were connected to the control room. They check the bulbs in warning lights, and test the recording machines to make sure the tapes were running smoothly.

THE INCIDENT ROOM

The police have set up an 'incident room' back at their headquarters. Everything in this room is to do with the robbery. The detectives meet to discuss the evidence they have found so far. Comparing the written statements, the videotape and the electronic record reveals one very puzzling fact. There were only 40 seconds between the first sound of the digger's engine and the moment when the guards rushed into the exhibition room. How did the robber break in and take the mask in just 40 seconds?

TV NEWS

Interviewed on TV, the police chief states that "Our enquiries are continuing and we are following a number of useful leads." She knows the robber may be watching. She wants the robber to feel unsafe.

Wednesday May 6th. The police team comprises of three police officers in the forensic team, three carrying out interviews, one detective in overall charge and up to seven other police officers following leads

CRIMINAL RECORDS

The police keep details – called criminal records – about all criminals who have been caught and punished. There are photographs of each person and a copy of their fingerprints and DNA profile, together with information about the crimes they have committed. How many criminals have robbed museums in this way before? Where were they last night? These people need to be questioned.

Detectives compare criminal records on computer monitors

The telephone rings all morning with the media requesting information

RED-HOT STORY

"Smash-and-grab with a digging machine! ... Mystery thief steals priceless golden Toltec Mask. ... Was museum raider a circus acrobat?" The media – newspapers, TV and radio stations – have turned the robbery into an exciting news story. The police chief does not tell them her suspicions about the exact time of the incident. She does not tell them about the screwdriver or that none of the fingerprints matches a known criminal. And she certainly does not admit that her team of detectives is at the moment puzzled by the crime.

TV RECONSTRUCTION

The TV station uses actors to film a reconstruction of the crime. Reporters know about the digger and the smoke grenades. They base their news reports on these simple facts. At the moment, the police are sure of very little; the media know even less.

"Who did it? Have you any leads? What are you doing about this?"

At noon the police chief reads a statement to the media; she refuses to answer questions

THE EVIDENCE SO FAR

Detectives always look for patterns which link things together. Here is a summary of all the clues collected so far. Using these clues, what can you say for certain about the robber? Try to describe the sort of person the police should be looking for.

1. Blood on glass fragment under window. It is blood group O, which is common throughout the world.
2. No DNA profile match with records of known criminals.
3. Clear fingerprint on screwdriver found next to glass with blood on it.
4. Robbery time 3.30 am.
5. Duration of crime is 40 seconds.
6. Distance of window to exhibition case: 3 metres.
7. Distance of window to ground: 4 metres.
8. Shoe imprint: size 42; shoes made in central America.
9. Smoke grenades: made in the USA.

Pressing an inked finger onto paper to make a print

A POSSIBLE SUSPECT

Could a criminal have come specially into the country to steal the mask? Detectives send descriptions of the robbery to Interpol – the International Police Commission. Interpol shares information about crimes among the police forces of different countries. It helps to catch international criminals who move from one country to another. Interpol sends out a message to each national police: "Does this robbery match any in your country? Can you think of any suspects who travelled recently from your country to another?"

TAKING FINGERPRINTS

"Just eliminating you from our enquiries, madam." While the museum staff were arranging the exhibition, they left their fingerprints everywhere in the room. The police use ink pads and paper to copy everyone's fingerprints. Experts at the fingerprint library quickly identify prints left by museum staff. Do the prints of one of the guards match the print from the screwdriver? Do they match prints from the brass handrail round the display cabinet? Decide if you think this guard is a suspect.

Tuesday May 5th. The police take copies of the museum staff's fingerprints to eliminate them from the enquiry

Faxed images of international criminals

Faxed image of the chief suspect

INTERNATIONAL CONNECTIONS

Fax machines are very useful. They can send writing and pictures along ordinary telephone lines. The police in Central America have received details of the mask robbery from **Interpol**. There have been several unsolved robberies from museums there. The police send details to Interpol about their chief suspect – someone they have never quite managed to catch red-handed.

FAX MACHINES

On the first machine, rollers pull the printed paper over a scanner. A tiny bright light moves back and forth across the moving paper. The light reflects from the image into a photocell, which generates an electric current. The current goes down the phone line to a second fax machine, which scans across blank paper, building up the image line by line.

The fingerprint library is in a computer database which will sort out similar type

Image printing at the receiving fax machine.

MAKING THE BREAKTHROUGH

One of the detectives is stirring a cup of coffee. He has been sorting through piles of evidence for hours. Suddenly he picks up the fax from the Central American police. "I saw that face two days ago!" And on the video of the TV news programme of the opening of the exhibition – there he is! Emilio Zapotec, a member of the team that brought the mask to the museum.

Thursday May 7th 6.30 pm. Zapotec "helping police with their enquiries"

The arresting police officer shows Zapotec his identification badge.

APPREHENDING THE SUSPECT

Zapotec is staying at a nearby hotel. It is time for the police to ask him some questions about the robbery. Policemen wearing ordinary clothes enter the hotel. They do not want to frighten other guests or give Zapotec the chance to run away. They ask him to come to the police station to help with their enquiries.

MAKING AN ARREST

Zapotec refuses to come to the station. Since the police are reasonably confident that he is mixed up in the crime, they arrest him. They caution him that anything he says may be taken as evidence in **court**. They can only keep him at the police station for 24 hours. Then they must charge him or let him go.

Just in time – Zapotec was just about to check out of the hotel.

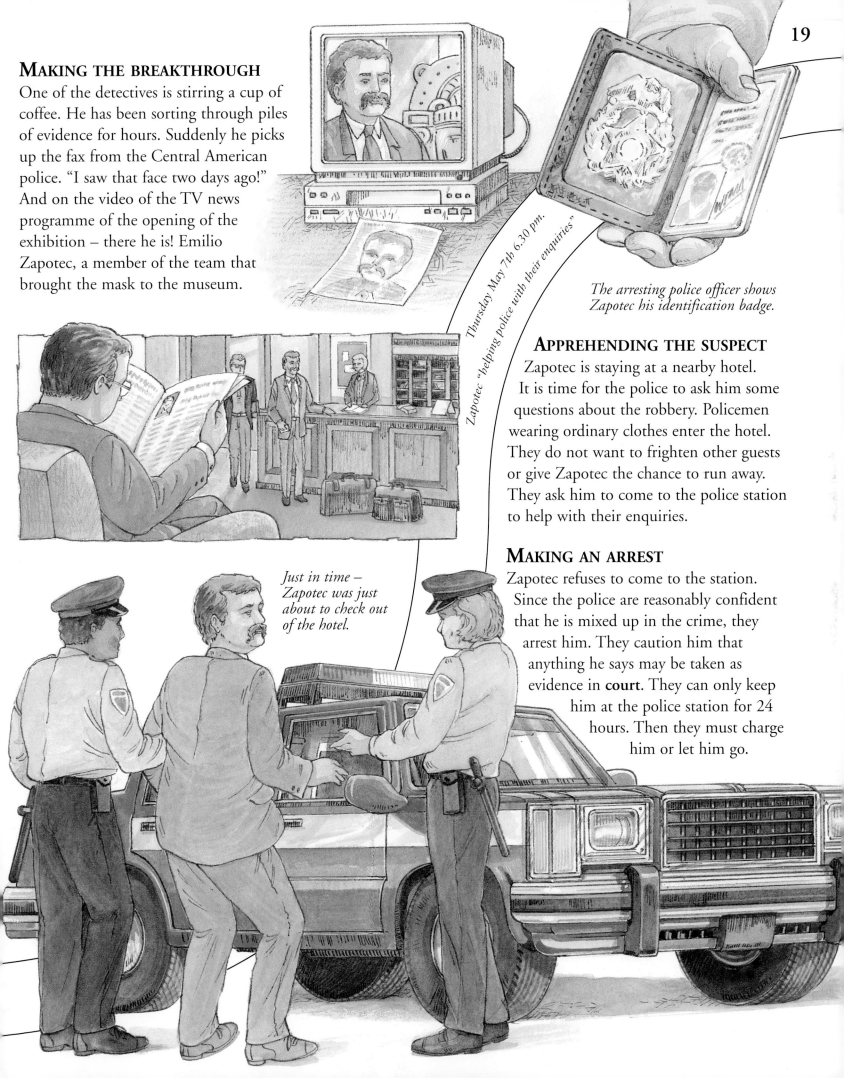

WHERE WERE YOU ON THE NIGHT OF THE 4TH?

Two police officers question the suspect. "Where were you between midnight on May 4th and 6 am on the morning of May 5th?" … "How did you cut your finger?" The legal expert tells Zapotec how to answer the questions. It is easy to fall into a trap unless you know exactly what each question means. The tape recorder holds two cassettes which run together. The police keep one cassette and the suspect keeps the other. Two identical recordings make sure that nobody can lie about what was said.

Strands of DNA make up genes

Zapotec's fingerprint

Fingerprint on screwdriver

Pairs of genes control each of your characteristics e.g. eye and hair colour

ANY MORE CLUES?

Even when hunting criminals, the police cannot do just as they like. Police officers and the forensic team must have permission to search the suspect's room. A local **judge** signs a search warrant. She is satisfied that the evidence against Emilio Zapotec is strong enough. At Zapotec's hotel room, the officers and team find newspaper articles about the Toltec Mask and about the security arrangements and building work at the museum. And under the bed are a pair of shoes made by the El Castillo Boot Company!

MATCHING FINGERPRINTS

Emilio Zapotec has no **alibi** for the time when the robbery happened. He cannot prove he was asleep in bed all night. The evidence is mounting against him. His shoes match the footprint found near the digger. Do you remember the screwdriver found under the window? His fingerprints are all over its handle!

Millions of separate genes combine to form thread-like chromosomes

Computers are used to compare DNA profiles.

TAKING A DNA SAMPLE

There is a drop of blood on the broken glass. A DNA profile will tell if it came from Zapotec. The doctor gently wipes inside Zapotec's mouth with a swab to collect loose skin cells. At the centre of each cell is a part called the **nucleus**. Coiled up inside the nucleus is the DNA. Every cell in a person's body contains exactly the same DNA. At the scientific laboratory, the DNA is extracted from the skin cells and analyzed using various chemicals.

Thursday May 7th. The police chief gives an interview to a television crew. It takes 20 minutes to record, but lasts just 30 seconds on the evening news

BIG PROBLEMS!

Like everything else in the Universe, DNA is made up from tiny particles called atoms. About 100 million atoms side by side would cover the width of your finger nail. The atoms in DNA are arranged in a pattern like coloured beads on a necklace. Different people have different patterns. Did the drop of blood come from Zapotec? No, it did not!

A TRICKY INTERVIEW

Ever since the robbery, the police chief has said almost nothing to newspaper reporters or to TV and radio interviewers. Now she tells them only the facts that are absolutely true. "We have arrested and are questioning Mr. Emilio Zapotec, who is a member of the trade delegation which brought the Toltec Mask to this country. We have evidence which links him to the theft of the mask."

Each cell in every human being has 46 chromosomes arranged in 23 pairs

WAS HE FRAMED?

This detective is puzzled. His job is to look at the tapes recorded from the security cameras at the museum. While re-examining the exhibition room tape, he has noticed a small fuzzy blob on the screen. It flies round and round the display cabinet which contains the mask. Then, as the time index on the picture ticks away five minutes, the blob seems to be frozen in mid-air. The next thing the detective sees on the screen is the digger bucket smashing through the window. Then the room fills with smoke.

Friday May 8th.

Details of the blob on the television screen, enhanced by computer

Radio receiver unit

Computer memory chip

The detective has a "hunch" that something is wrong with the videotape

THE FUZZY BLOB

A TV picture is made up from spots of light on the screen. A computer can store a picture by turning the brightness and position of each spot into a string of numbers. By adjusting the numbers, the computer can make the image sharper. The fuzzy blob was a moth. But how did it stay still for five whole minutes?

THE ELECTRONIC CULPRIT

Somebody has added this radio-controlled switch to the electronic circuits in the control room. It contains a receiver tuned to pick up a signal from the burglar's transmitter. There is also a computer **memory chip** which stores one complete picture from the TV camera. The videotape recorded a signal from the chip, not from the security camera. An electronics expert opens up and tests the radio-controlled switch.

DISMANTLING THE HARDWARE

The radio-controlled switch turns off the infra-red beams guarding the exhibition room and also makes the video tape recorder ignore the signal from the camera. During the robbery, for five minutes the tape recorded the last image scanned by the camera before the radio signal arrived. So the digger bucket smashed the window after the robbery happened and not before!

Electronics experts find the added secret circuit board

FINDING A CONNECTION

Who fitted the secret switch? The detectives ask all the museum staff: "Did anything unusual happen over the past few weeks?" One of the staff remembers seeing a new video camera technician outside the security room. The security equipment is checked every three months. The technician who called last week was not the usual person. He said it was a special visit. The detectives search the older videotapes and hope to find a picture of the new technician.

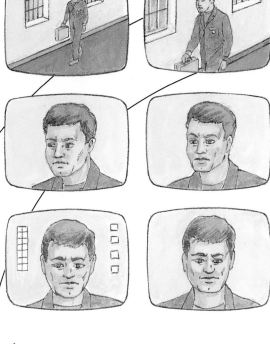

3.30pm. The bogus technician is identified from the videotapes

A NEW SUSPECT

Here is the bogus technician – the new suspect – walking down the main corridor. The TV picture is not very clear. The detective feeds the clearest image into the computer. The chief security officer met the bogus visitor and talked with him. The detective alters the image on the screen until the officer is convinced it looks exactly like the man he remembers.

The computer's 'photofit' software gives a range of shapes and colours of eyes, hairstyles and other facial features from which to choose.

THE CHASE IS ON!

The evidence against Emilio Zapotec is rather strange. The drop of blood did not come from him, but the fingerprints on the screwdriver did. The footprint matches his shoe. But does it connect him to the crime? The police now have a new lead. They are sure the mysterious visitor sabotaged the security system. The national TV station broadcasts the picture of the wanted man. "Have you seen this person?"

1873 · 0010

NATION-WIDE ALERT

The picture of the new suspect is everywhere – on TV and in the newspapers. People from all over the country telephone the police. Each person is sure they have seen the wanted man – on a bus, at the local supermarket, or in the park. There are hundreds of calls and the police must check every story.

Friday May 8th. Television broadcasts picture of the new suspect.
The videotape and the guard helps put together a photo fit

MR JONES'S HIDEAWAY

Mrs Cravat remembers the day that Mr Jones arrived. He told her that he was a film technician spending a few days in the area. In fact, he was looking for a quiet hideaway in a private house. During the day, he used his job to spy around the museum. At night he organized the plans for the robbery.

POSITIVE IDENTIFICATION

Mrs Cravat lives alone in a secluded house. She recognizes the face shown on last night's TV news. She is even more sure next morning when she opens her newspaper. Mrs Cravat telephones her local police station. "I'm sure the picture is of that nice Mr Jones who rented my spare room for a short time. Funny thing though: he disappeared the day before this picture was shown on the TV". Can this be the breakthrough?

8.30pm. The programme is broadcast

THE EVIDENCE MOUNTS

In Jones's lodging room, the forensic team find in a cupboard the overall seen on the museum video. They also find another pair of shoes made by the El Castillo Boot Company. There is soil trapped between the wavy grooves on the heel. Later, in the forensic laboratory, scientists find that the soil matches the sample taken from the scene of the crime. Finally, in a drawer, the forensic team find some electronic components and a complicated wiring diagram drawn on a piece of paper.

At passport control at the airport, an official matches Jones's photo with one of the images of wanted people on the computer screen.

Saturday May 9th. Mrs Cravat phones the police.
Mr. Jones is arrested at the airport

ELECTRONIC CLINCHER

Does the wiring diagram match the bogus equipment found at the museum? A skilled electronics engineer compares them and the answer is – "Yes".

FLIGHT DELAYED

Mr Jones did not see the TV programme and thinks he has fooled everyone. But officials at every airport have seen his picture and are looking out for him. He is caught trying to leave the country. At baggage check-in, an official finds $30,000 hidden inside the lining of Jones's suitcase.

WHAT ACTUALLY HAPPENED?

Mr Jones has told the police all about the robbery. He knows that he will spend less time in prison if he helps them find the stolen mask. The mastermind was the curator of the museum. He stole the mask to sell to a criminal art collector. The collector had also hired Zapotec to steal the mask.

Mr Jones and the curator plotted to raid the museum before Zapotec and leave evidence to incriminate him. Everything went according to plan – until the detective spotted the moth on the video film.

Saturday May 9th, Mr Jones makes a full confession at the police station

TRACKING THE CULPRITS

The police raid the curator's home, but he is not there. They track him down by locating his mobile phone. All mobile phones give off a continuous radio signal so they can lock onto the nearest relay station. The phone company can pick up this signal to locate a phone to within 100 metres. The curator keeps his mobile phone hidden in his jacket pocket.

FOOLING THE SECURITY SYSTEM

The robbery started when the curator pressed the button on the radio transmitter. The radio signal flipped the hidden electronic switch in the control room. For three minutes, the infra-red beams guarding the mask were switched off and the video recorder ignored the security cameras. The cameras switched on again just before the digger rammed the window. For a few seconds, the electronic memory chip continued to add the earlier picture, making it appear the mask was still in its case.

1 The curator transmits the signal to disable the alarms and freeze the security camera picture at 3.25 am.

2 He sticks a magnet to the door frame to hold the reed switch closed and enters the exhibition room.

3 At 3.26 am the guard in the control room sees nothing on the screen and no alarms sound.

4 Also at 3.26 am the curator breaks open the show case and steals the mask.

5 At 3.29 am he leaves the room, shuts the door and removes the magnet, moving swiftly back to hide in his office.

THE SCREWDRIVER FINGERPRINTS

Where did the incriminating fingerprint come from? Mr Jones was working as a technician for the TV crew at the opening ceremony. While pretending to fix a light, he held out the screwdriver to Zapotec. "Could you hold this for me a minute?" .... "Oh – OK" Can you think why Mr Jones is wearing thin cotton gloves?

PARTNERS IN CRIME

Mr Jones and the curator carried out the robbery together. They had to complete each step at exactly the right time. Earlier that day they had synchronized their watches so that they both showed precisely the same time. When Mr Jones was waiting in the digger, his watch told him when the security equipment switched off and when the curator was stealing the mask. The curator's watch told him how long until the cameras switched on again and when Mr Jones would come crashing through the window.

The partners in crime did not see each other at all during the robbery, so the curator was unaware that Mr Jones had left behind not only the screwdriver – deliberately – but also bloodstains, dirt from his shoes and footprints.

The curator and art collector are arrested: the Toltec Mask is recovered

6 Thirty seconds later, Mr Jones starts the digger engine. He smashes the window just after the cameras switch on again.

7 He throws in the smoke grenades, climbs the digger arm and drops in the screwdriver – but cuts himself on the broken glass.

8 Mr Jones drops to the ground. He runs away, leaving the distinctive footprints behind him.

STANDING TRIAL – THE EVIDENCE

It is six months since the robbery. The curator, the art collector and Mr Jones have all come to the court for their trial. Mr Jones pleads 'guilty'. He has told the police all about his part in the crime. The other two plead 'not guilty'. Their defence lawyers will speak for them, saying that they rescued the mask from Jones – clearly a lie! The prosecution lawyers will tell the story to make it appear as bad as possible. The judge makes sure that the trial is fair, and the twelve ordinary people in the jury will decide which story they believe.

THE TRIAL BEGINS

The **prosecution lawyers** bring in all the evidence collected by the police. This evidence includes items found in the museum and in Mr Jones's room, together with the results of scientific tests. Mrs Cravat and other witnesses will tell their part of the story. They will be carefully questioned by the prosecution and **defence lawyers**.

Jones faces charges of conspiracy, taking a vehicle without consent, and criminal damage

The curator faces charges of conspiracy, thefts, and criminal damage

The art collector faces charges of conspiracy and receiving stolen goods

THE FIRST EVIDENCE

The police detective holds up a powerful magnet and a reel of sticky tape found in curator's desk. The tape matches a small piece found on the exhibition room door frame. The curator's lawyer laughs: "Can you prove the curator stuck the magnet to the door frame? Did anybody see him do it?"

FINGERPRINT EVIDENCE

The fingerprint expert, called by the prosecution lawyers, tells the judge and jury that she found Zapotec's fingerprints on the handle of the screwdriver. But the position of the prints show that Zapotec simply held the handle with his fingers. The expert says that Zapotec's palm print would also be on the handle if he had used the screwdriver to break open the mask display case.

DNA EVIDENCE

The **forensic scientist** gives his evidence to the judge and jury. He shows how DNA profiling proves that the blood on the broken glass came from Jones. The problem is that Jones has pleaded guilty. His confession blames the curator and the collector but this story could be untrue. All the evidence so far points to Jones and not to them.

THE ELECTRONICS EXPERT

The **electronic diagram** found in Jones' bedroom matches the circuit board hidden in the control room. However, this expert witness also added: "Inside the lid of the box we found a fingerprint from the curator's thumb. There was also a hair which matches the collector's". Some of the bank notes hidden in Mr Jones' suitcase had fingerprints from the art collector.

Jones must spend four years in prison; the art collector two years and the curator six years

All three are found guilty!

THE FINAL VERDICT

The evidence and the speeches are over. The prosecution lawyer says that the evidence proves the men are guilty. The defence lawyers try to explain the evidence in a different way to make the curator and the collector appear innocent. The members of the jury have discussed the case for five hours. At last they have decided which story they believe and return to the court room. The **jury foreman** stands up to give the verdicts ....

Glossary

Alibi
Proof that you were somewhere else when a crime happened.

Closed circuit television
Television cameras linked by wires to TV screens and video recorders usually in the same building.

Clue
A piece of information or an object which helps to identify how a crime happened or who did it.

Control room
The room which contains TV monitor screens and alarms connected to the surveillance equipment.

Court
The place where a trial happens, involving the suspects, judge, jury, prosecution, and defence lawyers.

Curator
The person in charge of a museum.

Defence lawyer
An expert in the law who tries to show that the evidence is not linked to the suspects.

Detective
A member of the police force who collects evidence and sorts through it to solve a crime.

DNA
A complicated chemical found coiled up inside the nucleus of every living cell.

DNA profile
A pattern of bands made from a person's DNA. Each person has their own distinct pattern.

Electronic wiring diagram
Lines and symbols drawn on paper which show how to connect up the parts to make an electronic device.

Evidence
Clues and other facts which help to show that a person did or did not carry out a particular crime.

Fax
A machine which scans writing or pictures and sends a signal along phone lines to another Fax machine which makes an exact copy. 'Fax' is a shortened form of the word 'facsimile', which means a copy of something.

Fingerprint
An almost invisible pattern made from sweat and grease on fingertips which is left behind on a smooth surface. Each person leaves their own particular pattern.

Fingerprint dusting
Coating surfaces with fine powder and then blowing gently. The powder sticks only to the fingerprints and shows up the pattern.

Fingerprint library
A collection of fingerprints taken from all known criminals and labelled with their names and photographs.

Fingerprint powder
A fine dusty powder like talcum powder used to make fingerprints show up.

Forensic scientist
A scientist who uses scientific equipment to collect clues and to examine them as evidence for use in a court of law.

Forensic team
The detectives who look for clues which can be used as evidence against criminals.

Fraud
Criminals pretending that someone else committed a crime when in fact they did it in order to deceive the police.

Incident room
The place at a police station where detectives collect clues together and meet to discuss ideas about solving a crime.

Infra-red beam
A narrow collection of infrared rays all travelling together in the same direction like the rays of light from a torch.

Infra-red rays
A type of light which is invisible to human eyes but which electric sensors can detect.

Interpol
Short for the International Police Commission, which shares information between the police forces of different countries.

Judge
A lawyer who is in charge of a court and makes sure the trial is fair. The judge will also choose a punishment to fit the crime.

Jury
Twelve ordinary people in a court who listen to all the evidence and decide if the suspects are guilty or innocent.

Jury foreman
One member of a jury chosen to speak for all its members.

Memory chip
The part of a computer which can store electronic signals making up a picture, writing, program instructions or other information.

Monitor screen
A TV screen which shows the view seen by a closed-circuit television camera or is the visual display unit of a computer system.

Nucleus
The central part of a living cell which contains DNA and other chemicals controlling the cell's activity.

Plaster cast
A copy of footprints or dents, made by pouring liquid plaster into the imprint and allowing the plaster to set.

Prosecution lawyer
An expert in the law who tries to show that the evidence is clearly linked to the suspects.

Reed switch
A switch made from two flat steel springs which click together when a magnet is nearby.

Security officer
A person whose job is to keep a building or objects safe.

Sensor
A mechanical or electrical device which senses when something happens. Sensors respond to some sort of change in the surroundings.

Smoke grenade
A canister which gives off large amounts of dense smoke when set off.

Statement
A report noting what each person saw or heard while a crime was happening. A statement may be spoken, recorded on audio tape, or written down.

Surveillance equipment
All the sensors, closed circuit TV cameras, monitor screens, and alarms which help security officers to survey, or watch, the whole of a building all the time.

Time index
Numbers giving the time and the date which are automatically added to the pictures from closed circuit TV cameras.

INDEX